Donated by We ☑ P9-AGR-064
1980-81

THE ODYSSEY

THE ODYSSEY
Selected Adventures
By Homer

Adapted by Diana Stewart
Illustrated by Konrad Hack

Raintree Publishers • Milwaukee • Toronto • Melbourne • London

Library of Congress Number: 79-24480

3 4 5 6 7 8 9 0 84 83 82

Printed in the United States of America.

Library of Congress Cataloging in Publication Data

Stewart, Diana.
  The Odyssey.

  SUMMARY: Retells in simple language five episodes
in the voyage of the Greek hero Odysseus from Troy to
his home in Ithaca.
  [1. Mythology, Greek] I. Homerus. Odyssea From Troy.
English. Selections. II. Hack, Konrad. III. Title.
PZ8.1.S8573Od   813'.5'4   79-24480
ISBN 0-8172-1654-5 lib. bdg.

CONTENTS

ODYSSEUS LANDS IN PHAEACIA

1

For ten years the Trojans fought bravely to save their city of Troy from the Greeks. But the goddess Athena gave the Greeks wisdom and cunning.

"Build a giant horse out of wood," she told them. "Hide your soldiers inside the horse and take it to the Trojans as a gift—a peace offering. Then when they open the gates and move it inside the walls of Troy, the soldiers can come out and capture the city."

The trick was successful. Troy fell to the enemy, and joyfully the Greeks sacked the city. They loaded their ships to take the great treasures of Troy back to their homes. They were so pleased with the riches they found that they made a grave mistake—they forgot to give thanks to the gods for their victory.

The gods were enraged! After all their help, the great heroes of Greece had forgotten them! They vowed to punish the victors for their crimes. They would make the journey home a time of suffering and trial.

One of the greatest of these Greek heroes was King Odysseus, ruler of the island of Ithaca. He was Athena's favorite because of his great wisdom and cunning, and she had been hurt most when he failed to praise her for her help. So she took her friendship from him and left him alone to face the dangers that awaited him.

But it was not Odysseus's fate to die. After many hardships, he was finally cast up on the island ruled by Calypso, a beautiful young spirit. When Calypso first saw Odysseus, she loved him and made him a prisoner on her island. She gave him ambrosia, the food of the gods, and at night she took him with her to her cave. But all day long he sat on the beach looking out to sea, and he cried with longing for his homeland.

In all, nine years passed after the end of the Trojan Wars.

From high up in their home on top of Mount Olympus, the gods looked down on Odysseus. Athena saw the tears in his eyes and the suffering on his face. At last, she forgave him. The time had come to give him his freedom. She went to her father, Zeus, chief of all the gods.

"Oh, Great Father Zeus," said Athena, "I need your help. The time has come to set Odysseus free."

"I would willingly help you, my daughter," Zeus replied. "In the past Odysseus has always been very generous in his gifts to the gods. He is the wisest of all humans. But Poseidon, the Lord and Ruler of the Sea, has not forgiven him for his crimes."

"Poseidon has gone on a journey away from Olympus. With your help, we can free Odysseus before he returns. The great Sea-god will not dare complain if you and the other gods join to help Odysseus."

"What would you have me do, my child?" Zeus asked.

"Send Hermes with a message to Calypso. Tell her that it is your wish that Odysseus be freed. She must listen to you."

So Zeus called his messenger, Hermes, and had him put on his shoes with golden wings. With these he could travel over water and land as fast as the wind. Down, down Hermes went from Olympus to Calypso's island to deliver his message to the spirit.

"Oh, Hermes, I love him!" Calypso cried when she heard the message. "I want him for my husband. I will ask the gods to make him immortal, and he can live here with me forever!"

"You have kept him prisoner here for seven years, Calypso," Hermes said sternly. "He does not love you.

7

Look how the tears run from his eyes. His wife Penelope has been waiting faithfully for him for many years, since he left for the war. He has a grown son he has not seen since he was a boy. He is needed back on Ithaca. Zeus commands that you send him home!"

Although Calypso's heart ached, she had no choice but to agree. Odysseus wept with joy when she told him the news. He took the great axe Calypso gave him and cut down twenty trees to form a raft. Smaller ones he used to make a mast. The spirit gave him the material also for a sail. And because she loved him, she gave him clothes, food and water for his journey, and directions so he would not get lost.

At last when everything was ready, Odysseus set out across the great sea. For seventeen days, all went well. The sea was calm and the wind filled the sail. On the eighteenth day, he saw land in the distance.

But Odysseus's troubles were not over. Poseidon was on his way back to Olympus. By chance he looked down over his sea and saw Odysseus on his raft. He was furious!

Quickly he caused the winds to blow and clouds to form. In moments a great storm began to churn the waters. Helplessly Odysseus clung to his raft, but the wind blew down his sail and the waves pounded against the wood. The raft began to break. With a cry, Odysseus dove into the sea and began to swim toward the distant land.

He would have surely drowned if Athena had not been watching over him. She saw his danger and waited for Poseidon to leave. Once the Sea-god had gone, she calmed the winds and the waters. For two days Odysseus swam on. At last his feet touched the sand of the beach. With his last strength, he pulled himself into the bushes that lined the shore. He dug a hole in the ground for a bed, covered himself with leaves, and fell into an exhausted sleep.

The next morning—when the rosy fingers of the goddess Dawn brought light to the world—a princess and her maids took their washing to the river near where Odysseus slept.

After the work was done, they bathed in the sea and played ball on the shore. The sound of their laughter woke Odysseus from his sleep. He peeked out from the bushes and saw the young women playing. What was he to do? He needed their help, but he knew he was an awful sight. His body was dirty from the sand and sea water, and his hair was long and tangled. Worst of all, he had lost all his clothes in the sea.

But Athena gave him wisdom. He broke off a large branch of leaves to cover his nakedness and slowly went out onto the beach.

"My Lady," he said to the princess, "your beauty blinds me! Are you a goddess or a mortal? Whichever you are, I ask for your pity. Your land saved me from death in the sea, and now I need your help. Will you tell me where I am, and how I can reach your city? The gods will surely bless you with happiness and a long life if you will help me."

At first the princess was afraid. But she listened to Odysseus and saw that he was a gentle man who could be trusted.

"I will help you, Stranger," she said. "You are on Phaeacia. My father is Alcinous, king of this island."

She went over to the bushes where the washing hung to dry and brought him clothes to wear.

"If you will follow me, I will take you to the palace," she said when he had dressed. "I know my father will help you."

Odysseus was very grateful. And while the princess went to bring the wagon and mules, he prayed to Athena to thank her for his rescue.

Odysseus followed the princess to the palace and knelt down at the feet of King Alcinous.

"Oh, Great King," he cried, "I am much in need of your help. For seven years I have been a prisoner of the spirit Calypso. Now my raft has been destroyed in the sea, and I have no way to reach my homeland!"

King Alcinous's heart was touched by these words.

"Rise, Stranger," he said. "Sit here at the table and eat and rest."

It had been several days since Odysseus had eaten, and he gratefully did as the king asked him. While he ate, King Alcinous called for a minstrel to bring his lyre and entertain his new guest and the chiefs and counsellors who sat with him.

The song the minstrel sang was a beautiful song. It told of how the great King Odysseus built the wooden horse and defeated the Trojans.

As Odysseus listened, his eyes filled with tears. He cried for those days long ago when he had been happy. He cried for his lost friends. He cried for the years that had passed since he had seen his homeland. But he was ashamed of his tears and turned his face away from the company of people. King Alcinous, however, saw the tears that fell from the stranger's eyes. With a clap of his hands, he silenced the musician.

"Thank you, Minstrel," the king said. "Your song is beautiful, but it has made our guest sad. Now, Stranger," he said to Odysseus, "the time has come for you to tell us your name and why you wander the earth alone."

"You have been very kind, my Lord. And I will gladly tell you my story. I pray that you will listen and take pity on me, for fate has been very cruel."

And so Odysseus began his tale.

ODYSSEUS AND THE CYCLOPS

2

This is the tale that Odysseus told King Alcinous and his company.

"First of all," Odysseus said, "let me tell you that I am Odysseus, King of Ithaca. I am the same Odysseus who helped to defeat the Trojans. After we had sacked the city of Troy and loaded our ships, we set sail for home. I had twelve ships in my fleet and many men.

"But Zeus did not look kindly on us. Our travel was cursed with storms and rough water. The storms took us off our course, and we had to stop often for food and fresh water.

"After many weeks at sea, we came to an untamed island where no men lived. Goats roamed freely and plants grew wild all around. There we anchored our ships. With our bows and arrows, we killed the animals and made a feast.

"The next morning as I sat on the shore, I saw another island nearby. I could see smoke rising, but I could see no sign of people. I took one ship and crew, and we crossed to the island to see what kind of people lived there. We would see if they were savages or good, god-fearing men who would help us find our way home.

"As we came near the island, we saw a huge cave up on the hillside. In front of the cave was a large wall made of stones. I took twelve men with me and left the others to guard our ship. We made our way up the hillside to the cave. When we entered it, we saw that it was the home of a giant.

"My men urged me to leave this giant's den, but I was curious to meet him. Perhaps he would give us some friendly gifts. We helped ourselves to some cheese in the cave and sat down to wait for the giant's return.

"Before long we heard the loud noise of his coming. To our terror, we saw that it was a Cyclops! The Cyclopes are a race of giants that have one large, round eye placed right in the middle of their foreheads. They do not live by any laws. Each Cyclops lives only for himself. He cares nothing about his neighbors.

"The sight of this monster frightened us so much that we hid in the back of the cave. From there we watched as he drove his herd of sheep into his home. When they were all in the cave, he lifted a giant stone and closed the entrance. My heart sank. It would take fifty men like us to move such a rock.

"One by one he milked his ewes. Next he lit a fire, and it was then that he saw us huddled at the back of the cave.

" 'Who are you?' he roared. 'Have you come to rob me?'

"Bravely I stepped forward.

" 'Sir,' I said, 'we are on our way back from the wars and have lost our way. We have come hoping you will help us. Zeus will surely bless you.'

" 'Zeus!' he bellowed. 'I care nothing for the gods. Why should I when we Cyclopes are bigger and stronger than they are?'

"Saying this, he reached out and grabbed two of my men. With a single sweep of his hand, he bashed their heads against the wall. Their brains spilled out onto the ground and their blood ran into the dirt. Like an animal he tore their bodies apart and stuffed them into his mouth for his supper. Not a bone or piece of flesh was left. Then he washed the meat down with fresh milk from his pail. Without another word, he stretched himself out among his sheep and went to sleep.

"I was enraged! I wanted to take my sharp sword and stab it into his chest. But I was also no fool. If I killed him,

we would still be prisoners behind the giant rock. Not all of us together would be strong enough to move it from the entrance. I had to wait and find a plan to save us.

"The next morning the Cyclops killed two more of my men for his breakfast. After he had eaten, he pushed the stone aside and took his sheep off to graze, replacing the rock behind him.

"Trapped alone in the cave, we had no time to mourn for our lost friends. I had hit on a plan that might save us.

"On one side of the cave was the trunk of an olive tree. The Cyclops must have been planning to use it for his staff. With my sword I cut away the branches and sharpened the end of it to a point.

"My men and I hid it underneath the dung that covered the floor of the cave and waited for evening to come. At last the Cyclops returned. Two more of my men he killed for his supper. Now was the chance I had been waiting for.

"Luckily, I had brought with me a goat skin filled with a sweet, delicious wine. I filled a cup and held it out to the giant. With a grunt he took it and drank it. He belched with pleasure.

" 'Give me more!' he ordered.

"I poured another cup and held it out, and once again he emptied the cup.

" 'Tell me,' he said, 'what is your name?'

" 'Cyclops,' I answered, 'my name is Nobody.'

" 'Well, Nobody, give me more of your wine and I will give you a present.'

"Again I filled the cup.

" 'What is the present?' I asked.

" 'Because you have given me this delicious wine, I will eat you last of all. That is your present, Nobody!'

"He began to laugh at his own joke, but the wine had now made him drunk. With a grunt, he slumped to the floor and fell into a dead sleep.

"Quickly my men and I uncovered the pointed staff we

had made from the olive tree. I put the sharp end into the hot coals until the green wood nearly caught on fire. Quietly we carried the pole to where the Cyclops lay.

"With one hard push, we drove the burning point into the Cyclops's single eye and twisted it deep. It made a sound like hot metal stuck into a pail of water. The blood began to boil around the burning wood. Smoke poured out, and the eyeball burst from the heat.

"The Cyclops gave a terrible cry that echoed around the cave. Quickly we hid in the back of the cave as he rose and pulled the pole from his blind eye. Blood gushed out, and he roared and bellowed from the pain.

"From outside the cave, we heard the sound of voices. His screams had awakened the other Cyclopes in the nearby caves.

" 'What is wrong?' they called. 'Is somebody trying to rob and kill you?'

" 'It is Nobody!' the Cyclops cried. 'Nobody is trying to kill me!'

" 'Then if it is nobody, let us go back to sleep! You must be sick, and that is your own problem! Pray to the gods!' they laughed.

"For the rest of the night the Cyclops sat moaning and groaning in pain. Then when morning came, he pushed the rock away to let his sheep out to graze. But he sat down at the entrance of the cave to catch us if we tried to slip out. He must have thought we were fools!

"Moving very quietly, I strapped three sheep together with willows from the Cyclops bed. Then I tied one man under the bellies of each group of three sheep. For myself I chose a giant ram. Under his belly I clung to his thick wool.

"The Cyclops let the sheep out a few at a time. Carefully he ran his huge hands over their backs as they came up to him. But the fool did not think to feel underneath. My ram was the last one to leave the cave. The Cyclops held him at the mouth of the cave for a moment.

" 'What, my pet ram! Why do you move so slowly behind the other sheep? Ah, you must miss your master's eye, which a villain and his vile companions put out, dulling my wits with wine. Oh, if only you could speak! You could tell me where that miserable Nobody is hiding.' So saying, he let the ram leave the cave. Quickly I let myself down and untied my men, and we were free of the cruel giant.

"Without a backward glance, we drove the sheep down the hillside to where the rest of the men and the ship were waiting. I wanted to weep for my lost friends who had been eaten by the Cyclops, but there was not time. We loaded all the sheep on our ship and set sail. But I was still very angry, and before we had gone far, I called out to the giant Cyclops.

" 'Cyclops!' I shouted. 'I have had my revenge on you! You deserve to be blind for eating your guests!'

"With a roar, the giant picked up a huge rock and threw it into the sea. It made such waves that we were almost washed back to the shore.

" 'Be quiet!' my men begged me. 'What good does it do to make him even angrier!'

"But I would not listen to their good advice.

" 'Cyclops!' I shouted again. 'If anyone asks how you lost your eye, tell them it was done by Odysseus, King of Ithaca!'

" 'Odysseus!' he wailed. 'I should have known! A seer warned me that you would make me blind! But I was expecting a tall, handsome man, full of a mighty power. How was I to know that the great Odysseus was a pale little runt of a man? I will send you to Hades, Odysseus. I am the son of Poseidon. He will listen to me! Oh, Father Poseidon!' the Cyclops prayed. 'Bring down your anger on this man Odysseus. Curse him so that all his crew will drown, and he will never reach his home on Ithaca!'

"The Cyclops continued to pray as we sailed to the island

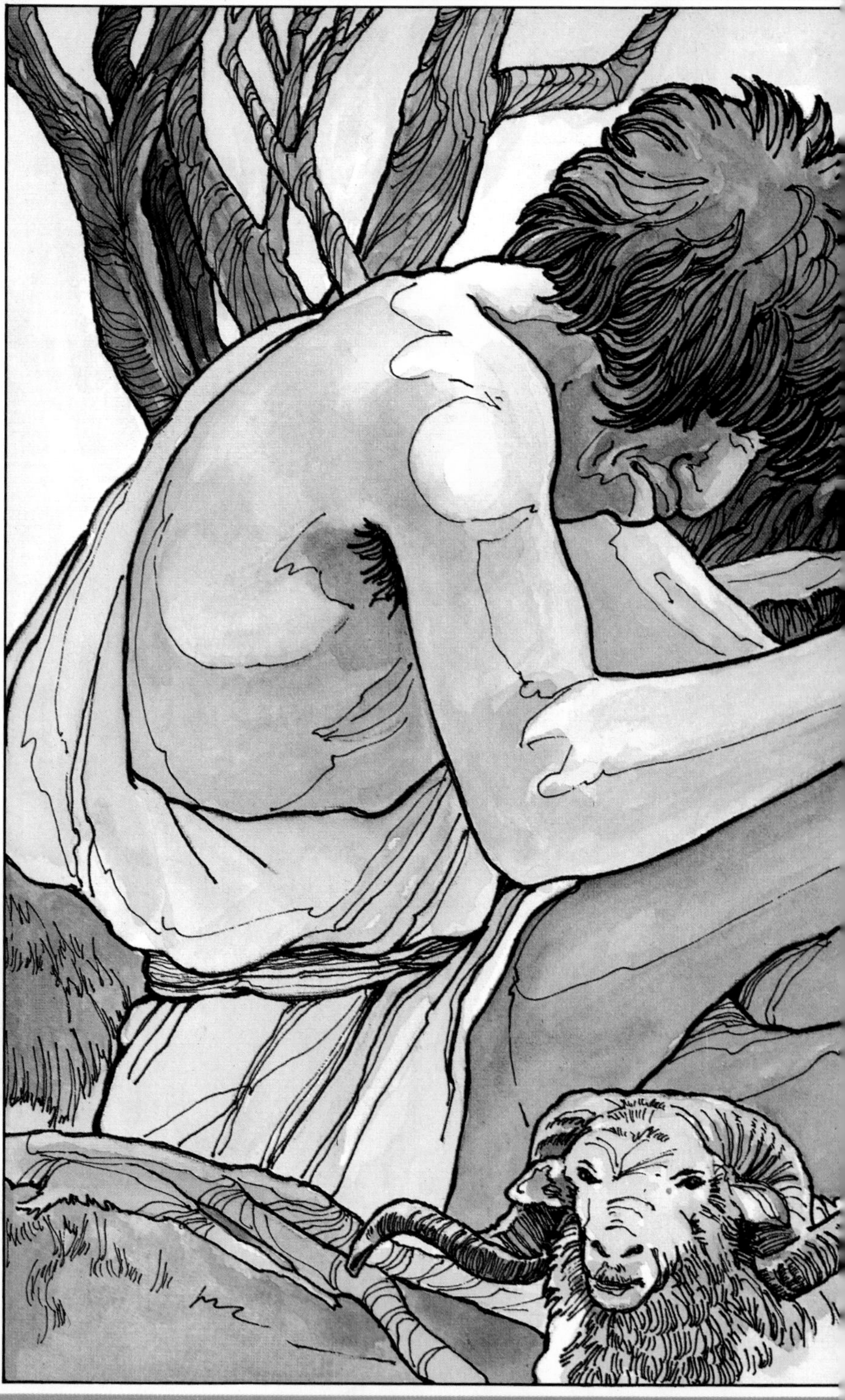

where the rest of our fleet was waiting for us. Our friends were overjoyed to see us safely back, but they cried for the men who had been lost.

"We divided the sheep we had taken. The giant ram I kept as a sacrifice to Zeus. But he was not listening to me. He was too busy planning the destruction of my men and fleet."

ODYSSEUS AND CIRCE

3

"For many days we sailed on. The next island we saw was the home of Aeolus, Keeper of the Winds. His was a friendly island. He and his family took us in and fed us and gave us a place to sleep. For a month we remained there, resting and regaining our strength after our hard adventures.

"But the time came to continue our journey. Before we left, Aeolus gave me a gift. It was a bag made from the skin of an ox. He had filled it with the Winds and tied it tightly so none could escape unless we needed them to fill our sails.

"For nine more days we sailed on. On the tenth day, the foolishness of my men brought us disaster!

"Ever since we left Aeolus, I had sailed the ship myself. I refused to sleep. On that tenth day, the land of Ithaca was in sight. At last I thought I could turn the ship over to my men and rest. But no sooner was I asleep than the men began to plot against me. They had seen Aeolus give me the leather bag and thought it was filled with gold and silver.

" 'Odysseus keeps this treasure for himself!' they said. 'He brings home friendly gifts, while we, who have worked as hard as he has, come home with empty hands. Come! Let us open the bag and divide the gold among ourselves.'

"As they cut open the pouch, all the Winds rushed out. Their force created a terrible storm, and the ship tossed

23

back and forth on the waves. Once more we were carried out to sea away from my beloved Ithaca.

"Oh, how my men wept and begged my forgiveness. I was so sick at heart that I cried and moaned for my lost homeland. But crying never does any good. We had to continue on.

"Many more storms and cruel adventures came upon us. Finally, only my own ship remained—all the others had been lost at sea. I had almost given up hope of ever reaching land again, when an island appeared in the distance.

"We landed and found food and fresh water to keep us going, but we still had no idea what direction to sail to reach Ithaca. Leaving my men on shore, I set off to explore the island. I took my spear and my sword and climbed the rocky hillside. From the top of one high hill, I could look down over the island. There in the center I saw smoke rising from among the trees and bushes.

"At first I was going to go down by myself, but I did not want to face the possible danger alone. Back at the ship, I divided my men into two scouting parties of twenty-two men each. I made one man captain of one group, and I took charge of the other. While we stayed to guard the ship, the other party went to explore.

"In time they arrived at the palace of Circe, a powerful goddess. Prowling all around the castle were tame mountain lions and wolves. My men did not know then that these were victims of Circe's black magic.

"The men were frightened by the animals and ran to the door of the house for protection. From inside they could hear the sound of a woman singing as she worked at her loom. When they called to her, she came to the door and invited them in. All but the captain of the group entered gladly. He did not trust the beautiful face and sweet voice of Circe.

"While he waited outside, the lovely witch seated the men at her table.

" 'Here,' she said. 'I have fixed food and wine for you. Eat, drink, and rest from all your labors and cares.'

"But in the food Circe put a powerful drug. As soon as the men ate and drank, they fell under her spell and lost all memory of their homeland. When all my friends were drugged, the witch touched them with her magic wand. In an instant they were turned into pigs. They not only looked like pigs with snouts and bristles, they also grunted like pigs.

"Then Circe drove them out of the castle and into the pig pens. There she left them to wallow in the mud. Tears ran from their eyes as they stood helpless in the pens, for their shapes had been changed, but not their minds.

"For hours the captain waited for his friends, but they did not come. At last he gave up hope and returned to me on the shore. He wept as he told me his sad story.

" 'Stay here with the rest of the men,' I ordered.

" 'You will die just like the others!' he cried, and he threw himself at my feet.

" 'It is my duty to go and find out what happened to my men,' I replied.

"I followed the track through the brush and trees. I had not gone far when I met Hermes disguised as a young boy, and he took my hand in greeting.

" 'I know where you are going,' he said. 'You want to find your comrades. But Circe has changed them into pigs, and you are likely to join them without my help.'

" 'You will help me?' I asked.

" 'Yes. Let me tell you how Circe works her black magic. She puts a poison into the food and wine she makes. This allows her to cast her spells with her wand. First, I am going to give you the drug of goodness. Take it now. This will keep the poison from working. Then, when she touches you with her wand, draw your sword and pretend that you mean to kill her. At first she will be frightened, but then her heart will soften, and she will ask to be your friend. Make her swear then that she will do nothing to hurt you in any way.'

"I listened carefully to everything Hermes told me and

took the drug he gave me. Then I went off in search of Circe's castle.

"All was just as my friends had found it. Circe sat singing at her loom, and when I called, she asked me to enter and eat with her. Carefully she brewed up the food mixed with her poison and watched me as I ate it. Then she took her magic wand and touched me.

"Quickly I drew my sword and turned on her, but she slipped under my blade and threw herself at my feet.

" 'You must be Odysseus,' she cried. 'I was told that no magic could defeat you, and that you would come to my island on your way home from the wars. Come and sit with me. We will talk and learn to trust each other.'

"I remembered the words of Hermes, and before I went with her, I made her swear that she would not harm me.

"Later we returned to the dining hall. A bath had been set for me before the fire. After I bathed, she gave me beautiful clothes to wear. Her maids set the table with all kinds of delicious food for us.

"But as I sat at the table, I could not eat. How could I when my friends remained in the pig pens outside?

" 'What is the trouble, Odysseus?' she asked. 'You look so unhappy and you do not eat.'

" 'Do not ask me to be happy when my friends are still under your spell,' I answered sadly. 'If you want me to eat and drink, you must free them.'

"Circe took her wand, and I followed her to the pig pens outside. She rubbed a lotion on the back of each of the pigs, and before my eyes the spell was broken. My friends stood before me looking younger and more handsome than ever. Oh, how we cried with joy!

"Yet we missed our friends back on the ship. So I returned to my swift ship and was greeted by the men, who ran forth and gathered around me in sorrow.

" 'Odysseus,' they cried, 'tell us about the loss of our friends.'

"I spoke softly, saying: 'Let us make safe our ship, and

then you may follow me to the magic house of Circe. There you will find your friends eating and drinking in good cheer.' At this the men rejoiced, and followed me to Circe's house, where they greeted their lost friends with tears of gladness.

"Even Circe's heart was touched by our reunion. From then on she was most kind to me and my comrades. She invited us all to join her and enjoy the comforts of her enchanted palace.

"This we did for a full year, until at last the time came for us to continue our journey back to Ithaca."

THE FOLLY OF ODYSSEUS'S MEN

4

"After a year had passed, Circe saw that we were determined to leave her beautiful island.

" 'I will not keep you against your will,' she said. 'But come with me, Odysseus, and I will tell you what troubles are ahead of you.'

"While my men slept, I sat with Circe and listened carefully to all she told me.

" 'Your travels will not be easy,' she said. 'There are many dangers that await you, but if you will heed my advice, you may yet return to Ithaca.

" 'The first danger you will meet comes from the Sirens. They sit high up on the rocks singing. Their song is so beautiful that it casts a spell over all sailors who hear it. That is the way they lure the men to their deaths. They sit and sing, surrounded by the bones and rotting flesh of poor sailors.

" 'To escape the Sirens, you must take softened beeswax. Have your men put it in their ears so that they cannot hear the evil song. If you yourself would like to hear it, have your friends strap you to the mast of your ship. Make sure the ropes are tied very tightly. If you beg them to let you go, they must tie you with even more ropes. Tell your men that they must sail past the Sirens's rocks as fast as they can. Then you will be safe.

" 'Once you have passed the Sirens, you will reach a place where you can take one of two ways. The choice is yours. One way is a narrow path through steep cliffs. There the waves pound so hard against the rocks that no ship can pass through without being dashed to pieces.

" 'The second path you can choose takes you between two rocks. On the one rock lives Scylla. She is a terrible monster with the bark of a dog. Her home is a cave high up on the rock. She has twelve legs that dangle in the air and six heads on the ends of six long necks. Each head has three rows of sharp teeth. Scylla hates all men, and as you go by, she will grab six of your comrades with each of her heads.'

" 'Can't we fight her?' I asked.

" 'Oh, Odysseus!' Circe cried. 'You are very brave, but sometimes you are very foolish! No one can kill Scylla. If you stop to fight her, she will take six more of your friends. You will not be a coward if you sail by her as fast as you can.'

" 'Isn't it possible to sail around her?' I asked.

" 'No. On the rock on the other side Charybdis lives. Her mouth is a great, wide hole. When she sucks the water in, she makes a giant whirlpool. No ship can escape it. Then three times a day, she spits the water back to the heavens. If you are caught in either the whirlpool or the spitting water, no one can save you. Your best way is to stay close to Scylla's rock. It is better for you to lose six of your men than your whole ship!

" 'Once you are safely by these two dangers, you will come to the Island of the Sun-god. Here he keeps seven herds of fifty cattle and seven flocks of fifty sheep. The Sun-god loves his animals. You and your men must not touch them. You must think only of getting home and remember that nothing else is important. If you do this, you will still meet other dangers, but you will arrive home safely. But if you or your men should kill the Sun-god's herds or flocks, I promise you that your ship and men will be destroyed. You yourself will not see Ithaca for a very long time!'

"Circe finished speaking, and Dawn once more touched the sky with light. The time had come for us to leave the

31

enchanted island. As we sailed away from Circe's home, I told my men about the Sirens and what we had to do to escape.

"I sent part of the men to row the ship onward, and we travelled at great speed. Taking a square of beeswax, I softened it between my fingers. Each man put it in his ears. Then my friends tied me to the mast with strong ropes. At last we drew near to the Sirens's rocks. Oh, I heard such sweet singing in my ears! I longed to stay and listen to the song.

" 'Come to us, great Odysseus,' the Sirens sang. 'We know all the secrets of the earth. We can make you wise and bring you great delight.'

"I cried out to my men to set me free, but they tightened the ropes and added more. They did not let me free until we were far away from the Sirens and all danger.

"We had not sailed for long before we saw before us the two great rocks of Scylla and Charybdis. I had not told my comrades about the danger that faced us here. If they knew, they might leave their oars to hide in the hold. Our only chance to escape was for them to row as fast as possible.

"As we watched, Charybdis vomited up the water around the rock. It shot high into the air. Then she sucked it back down again into her waiting mouth. My men trembled with fear, but I ordered them forward.

" 'Stay close to the rocks away from the whirlpool!' I called.

"Because they were watching Charybdis' swirling mouth, they did not see the terrible sight of Scylla's six heads sticking out of the cave above them. Without warning, she suddenly swooped down and gobbled up six of my friends. Their legs and arms dangled from Scylla's mouths as she carried them up to her hole in the rock. Their cries were horrible!

" 'Odysseus!' they cried, and my name was the last word they spoke. Scylla ate them there at the entrance to her cave. Never again do I want to see such a terrible sight! Our hearts were aching for our dead friends, but we sailed quickly on and out of danger.

"A few days later we reached the beautiful Island of the Sun-god. I remembered Circe's warning and called my men together.

" 'There is danger for us on that island,' I said. 'We will not stop there.'

"A great cry went up from my comrades.

" 'Odysseus, are you made of iron?' they said. 'We have been sailing for many days without rest! We need to anchor our ship and feel the solid ground under us. We need to cook a cheerful meal. Evening is coming on, and there is more danger to us from the winds that come at night. It is folly to continue on!'

"All my men were against me. I had no choice but to agree.

" 'All right,' I said. 'But you must give me your solemn oath that you will not touch any of the animals that roam the island. For if you do, it will surely mean the end of us all. We still have the food that Circe gave us. Eat only that, and do not wander away from the ship!'

"They gave me their promise, and happily anchored the ship. From a river nearby we got fresh water. On the beach we built a fire. And they kept their word and only used the food in our own supply. After the meal we wept for our lost friends whom Scylla had eaten and then fell asleep.

"Just before Dawn brought her light to the world, Zeus gathered the clouds together. A great storm began to blow and soon blotted out the sky. We pulled our ship into a quiet cove, and once more I warned my men.

" 'We must wait here until the storm passes, but we still have plenty left to eat. Do not touch the animals on the island, or it will mean our death!'

"Once again they promised, and we waited for the storm to pass.

"For a whole month the winds blew against us. There

was no hope of leaving the island. While our food lasted, my men did not complain. But at last the food and wine were gone. The men grew hungry and restless.

"One day I left them as they searched for fish and birds to eat. I went off for a quiet place to pray to the gods. I prayed to all the gods on Mount Olympus, but they did not listen. Instead, they put me into a deep sleep.

"While I was gone, my men rebelled. A leader among them told my friends his plan.

" 'My friends,' he said, 'we will starve to death if we listen to Odysseus. It would be better to drown quickly in the sea than to slowly starve to death. Let us gather together the best of the sheep and cattle for our food. Then when we get back home, we will build a temple to the Sun-god and ask his forgiveness.'

"I awoke from my sleep and returned to the ship. In the air I could smell the sweet smell of meat roasting. I looked at the dead sheep and cattle and fell on my knees in fear.

" 'Father Zeus!' I cried. 'You have done this to me! You put me to sleep so that I could not stop my men from killing the Sun-god's animals!'

"High up on Olympus the Sun-god came to Zeus.

" 'I want revenge on Odysseus's men for killing the sheep and cattle I loved!' he told Zeus. 'If you will not destroy them, I will take my light from the world and go down to Hades and let it shine there!'

" 'You shall have your revenge,' Zeus promised the Sun-god. 'I will bring them death and destruction!'

"My men feasted on the stolen cattle and sheep for six days. At the end of that time, Zeus calmed the storm. On the seventh day, we left the island behind us.

"The sea was calm for the first while until there was nothing but water all around us. Then Zeus sent the storms again—stronger and more fierce than ever. The wind tossed us on the water. The waves battered against the sides of the ship and spilled over the deck. Then Zeus

struck his final blow. He threw a lightning bolt that struck us with a terrible force.

"My men were thrown into the sea. They struggled helplessly in the churning water and were finally drowned—every one of them.

"I clung to the mast, but the ship broke apart underneath me. As the mast was thrown into the raging waters, I held on tightly and saved myself from the fate of my comrades.

"The storm had blown in from the west, but suddenly the wind changed and blew from the south. This meant that I would be carried back to the rocks of Scylla and Charybdis. All night long I was carried along by the pounding waves. When morning came, I saw the terrible sight of Charybdis's whirlpool.

"I thought my end had surely come, but just before I reached swirling waters, a wave flung me free of the mast and up onto the side of the rock. There I clung to a fig tree. I could find no foothold to rest my feet, and I hung there by the strength of my arms. My only hope was that Charybdis would vomit up the wood from my ship. My faith was rewarded! The next time Charybdis spit up the sea water, the mast was thrown back out into the sea. I dove into the water, swam to the mast, and began rowing as hard as I could with my arms. I was saved!

"For nine days I remained at sea. Then on the tenth, the gods brought me to the island of Calypso. And there I remained a prisoner for seven years until the gods in their mercy released me, and I made my way here."

And so Odysseus finished his tale.

ODYSSEUS RETURNS TO ITHACA

5

The company in the great hall at Phaeacia was amazed by Odysseus's story.

"You have indeed had an unhappy time," said King Alcinous. "We will do everything in our power to see that you return safely to your homeland."

The king ordered that a ship and crew be prepared for Odysseus, and he loaded it with costly gifts. When everything was ready, Odysseus thanked his host.

"Farewell, oh great King Alcinous," he said. "May the gods keep you from harm, and may you and your people find much happiness with your wives and children."

After many days at sea, the Phaeacians landed him at last on his beloved Ithaca. And in all, over nineteen years had passed since he left his home and family. Alone he stood on the shore, but the goddess Athena in her wisdom had covered the land with a mist so that Odysseus did not recognize it. Before he could return to his palace, she must warn him of the dangers that awaited him there. With her help, he might still live to a ripe old age with the comfort of his family around him. So she appeared to him in the disguise of a shepherd boy.

Tears had once again filled Odysseus's eyes. He did not know where the Phaeacians had gone, and he feared that he would never reach his home.

"Good day to you sir," said Athena.

"Hello, boy," Odysseus replied. "Will you tell me what land this is? I am a stranger here."

"Why sir," Athena replied, "this is the island of Ithaca."

"Ithaca!" Odysseus's heart leaped with joy.

Athena smiled at his pleasure and touched his hand. In an instant her form changed, and she stood before him in her own shape—as the goddess who had been his friend.

"Do you not recognize me, Odysseus?" she asked.

"Athena! It is hard for a man to recognize you when you appear in so many shapes. Is it true that I am really back on Ithaca?"

"It is true, Odysseus." And she lifted the mist so that he could see the land for himself.

He fell down on his knees and kissed the ground in joy.

"Rise, Odysseus," Athena commanded. "I must tell you of the dangers that face you at your palace.

"For over three years now, lords and princes from Ithaca and many neighboring lands have been living at your palace. They believe you are dead. So they come to woo your beautiful wife Penelope and demand that she choose one of them for a husband. But still she weeps for you and will not accept any of them. These suitors, however, are powerful men, and she does not dare turn them out of your home. So there at the palace they stay. They eat you out of house and home and waste your fortune. They have even plotted to kill your son, Telemachus.

"These fine lords and princes are a cruel and greedy bunch. If they knew you had returned, they would try to kill you, too. Therefore, you must return to the palace in secret and find a way to rid your house of these enemies."

"Tell me what to do, oh wise Athena. You have helped me in the past, and I will be guided by your words."

"Then go first to the old shepherd's hut. Wait there until I send your son to you. He has grown into a fine young man, and together you can plan the death of these suitors."

Athena touched Odysseus with her wand. In an instant he was changed into an old, wrinkled tramp. His clothes became rags, and his shoulders were stooped. Now he could make his way across the island without being recognized.

40

Odysseus left the goddess and made his way through the hills and woods until he came to the hut. There the old shepherd took him in and gave him food and rest. The next morning when Telemachus arrived, Athena once more changed the king into his normal shape. The father and son wept with happiness at their reunion.

"You know about the suitors who want to marry my mother?" Telemachus asked.

"Yes!" Odysseus exclaimed.

"They are our enemies and will do anything to steal your wife and fortune away from you. It will take all your brains and strength to defeat them."

"Then do as I say, Telemachus. Go back to the palace. I will come later dressed as the ragged tramp. Demand that I be allowed to stay and beg for food. I must see these men for myself."

Telemachus obeyed his father, and when Odysseus arrived at the palace door dressed as a beggar, his son invited him in. Most of the suitors feared that this stranger might be a god in disguise and shared their food with him. One suitor, however, the greediest and cruelest of them all, cursed him and threw a stool at him to drive him off.

When Penelope heard how the stranger had been treated by her guest, she commanded that the beggar be brought to her.

"Stranger," she said when Odysseus knelt before her, "you have been many places in your travels. Tell me, have you heard any news of my husband, Odysseus?"

"I have, my Queen," he answered. "He is not dead as many people tell you. He is alive and not far from Ithaca."

"Oh, if only I could believe you!" the beautiful Penelope cried. "My suitors are pressing me to choose a husband quickly. For three years I put them off. I told them that I was weaving a funeral robe for Odysseus's father. I said that I would not marry until the robe was done. All day I worked at my loom, but each night I undid all the weaving I had done during the day.

42

"All went well until a servant woman caught me one night. She told a lord—who was her lover. When my suitors found that I had been making fools of them, they demanded that I choose my new husband. I am afraid that I must choose soon. They are powerful men."

"You must wait, Queen Penelope!" Odysseus told her firmly. "I tell you that Odysseus will be here soon to rid his house of these enemies. Until then, the gods will surely help you."

That night Athena put a plan into Penelope's mind. The next day the queen went to the secret room where Odysseus kept his weapons. There she took his great bow. It had been a gift from a beloved friend, and only he was strong enough to string the bow. Down to the hall she went with the great bow and a quiver of arrows.

"My lords and princes!" she said to the suitors. "The time has come for me to choose a husband. I will marry the man who can put the string in Odysseus's great bow and shoot an arrow through twelve axes put together in a row."

Odysseus sat in the corner of the room and watched as one suitor after another tried to string the bow—and failed!

"Telemachus," he called softly to his son. "Order the women to go to their rooms and lock their doors. Then bar the great door at the end of the hall. Next, go to my rooms and bring me my sword and shield!"

Telemachus hurried to obey his father, and Odysseus rose to his feet.

"None of you are men enough to take the place of Odysseus!" he cried. "Even a man as old and feeble as I am can string the great bow!"

He took the bow from an angry suitor and strung it easily. Then he took an arrow and shot it through all twelve of the axes. The crowd of men watched in amazement. They did not see him take another arrow and fit it into the bow. He drew back the arrow and shot it through the neck of the suitor who had been so cruel to him.

"What are you doing!" the others cried.